CHEVY PICKUP TRUCKS

Steve Statham

Motorbooks International
Publishers & Wholesalers®

First published in 1996 by Motorbooks International
Publishers & Wholesalers, 729 Prospect Avenue, PO
Box 1, Osceola, WI 54020-0001 USA

Motorbooks International is a certified trademark,
registered with the United States Patent Office

The information in this book is true and complete to
the best of our knowledge. All recommendations are
made without any guarantee on the part of the author
or Publisher, who also disclaim any liability incurred in
connection with the use of this data or specific details

We recognize that some words, model names and
designations, for example, mentioned herein are the
property of the trademark holder. We use them for
identification purposes only. This is not an official
publication

Motorbooks International books are also available at
discounts in bulk quantity for industrial or sales-
promotional use. For details write to Special Sales
Manager at the Publisher's address

Library of Congress Cataloging-in-Publication Data
Statham, Steve,
     Chevy pickup trucks / Steve Statham.
       p. cm. -- (Enthusiasts color series)
     Includes index.
     ISBN 0-7603-0103-4 (pbk. : alk. paper)
     1. Chevrolet trucks--History. I. Title. II.
     Series.
     TL230.5.C45S73   1996
     629.223--dc20   96-14053

On the front cover: Chevrolet's Cameo Carrier pickups
were among the first to adopt car-type creature comforts
and styling features. This 1957 model is owned by Art
Hunter of Austin, TX.

On the back cover: The trucks of the 1930s reflected
the same art deco influences as the architecture and
popular art of the time. Shown is a 1939 half-ton
owned by Mike Wilson of Georgetown, TX.

On the frontispiece: Detail of a 1956 Cameo Carrier,
owned by Bernard and Mary Meyer of Wylie, TX.

On the title pages: This 1968 C-10 is owned by Pete
Farmer of Austin, TX.

Printed in Hong Kong

CONTENTS

ACKNOWLEDGMENTS

No book project, even a relatively small one such as this, is ever completed without the help and assistance of a variety of knowledgeable individuals. My thanks go out to those who contributed by sharing their time or knowledge, starting with Chip Sweet with the Vintage Chevrolet Club of America, and Anne Cook, librarian with the Texas Department of Transportation. Thanks are also due Augie Holtkort and Dale Mayeaux for their assistance in locating suitable trucks to photograph, and Paul Zazarine for last-minute help locating photography.

Some established texts were invaluable resources for information, such as *75 Years of Chevrolet*, by George H. Dammann, and *The Standard Catalog of American Light Duty Trucks*, edited by John Gunnell.

Normally, it's necessary to travel from one end of the country to the other to find and photograph all the vehicles needed to fill the pages of a book like this, but, true to its reputation as the No. 1 truck market in the known universe, I was able to find virtually every truck featured in these pages in Texas. Special thanks go to these fellow Texans. They are:

Bob Blackwell, Austin, 1928 Chevrolet truck; Jerry Corona, Austin, 1961 Corvair 95 Rampside pickup; Pete Farmer, Austin, 1968 C-10; Paul Garlick, Lehigh Acres, Florida, 1961 Apache C-10; Lester Gaylor, Wylie, 1957 Cameo Carrier; Honda Heath, San Antonio, 1972 Cheyenne Super 10 (with extra thanks to son Brandon Heath and Harley Spaulding in Oklahoma); Art Hunter, Austin, 1957 Cameo Carrier; Edwin and Leatrice Koehler, San Antonio, 1949 3100 Pickup; Don McElwreath, Cedar Park, 1971 Suburban; Bernard and Mary Meyer, Wylie, 1956 Cameo Carrier, 1957 GMC Suburban, 1957 Chevy 1-ton, 1958 Cameo Carrier; Carl Van Roekel, New Braunfels, 1970 El Camino SS396 (with special thanks to Frank Kalson for his assistance); Ronnie Stokley, Humble, 1965 C-10; Forest "Chip" Sweet, Lake Jackson, 1931 Fire Truck, 1932 Roadster Pickup; and Mike Wilson, Georgetown, 1939 Pickup.

Early Chevy trucks were models of simplicity. After decades of service, this 1928 model awaits restoration.

INTRODUCTION

Why is Chevy's workhorse pickup such a celebrated part of America's industrial heritage? There are many reasons, not the least of which is that a Chevy truck is simply a good product. But there are a lot of good products in the marketplace, and you rarely find the kind of near-fanatical loyalty Chevrolet pickups engender transferred to specific brands of VCRs, pencils, or refrigerators. All are items used daily, but usually the choice of which to purchase comes down to who has the lowest price. Clearly, just making a good product isn't enough.

People remain loyal buyers of Chevy trucks because the pickups have earned that right. The life of a pickup is often tough, and if it holds up to the countless abuses people heap on their vehicles, it achieves a new status. After a truck has proven itself reliable as transportation and a hard worker, it moves up the product-loyalty ladder and becomes less a piece of machinery and more a part of the family. A faithful pickup achieves roughly the same status as a loyal dog, and for many of the same reasons. (A pickup may even achieve higher status than the family dog, since it will, for example, never pee on the carpet. But to be fair, a dog will never leak oil on the driveway.)

People appreciate the kind of vehicle that will serve them well through good times and bad, in all conditions, and through so many of life's stages. Therefore, it's no surprise that the full-size truck market is one of the last bastions of true owner loyalty. It's still not unusual to run across the sentiment, "By God, granddad drove a Chevy truck, papa drove a Chevy truck and I drive a Chevy truck."

Sales of Chevy trucks have run the gamut. Chevrolet started, like virtually all other American car manufacturers, in the shadow of Henry Ford. The first Chevy truck chassis went from being just another puny challenger to Henry's Model T to the best selling truck in the land in the span of one decade. Chevrolet then ruled the roost through most of the middle years of this century. In a top sales year, such as 1978, Chevy moved 731,914 full-size pickups out the door, plus vans, medium- and heavy-duty trucks, El Caminos and LUV compact trucks. Here at the end of the millennium Ford has re-established itself as the industry leader, although when GMC and Chevy truck sales are combined, they usually best Ford.

Strong truck sales and strong Chevrolet owner loyalty are not likely to end soon. Trucks constituted just 12.5 percent of industry market share in 1960. In 1994, trucks accounted for 41.7 percent of total sales. People who like having a loyal truck wagging its tail in the driveway more often than not choose a Chevy.

Trucks of the thirties were known for bold styling and distinctive, art deco grille designs. Shown is a 1930 model.

BETWEEN THE WARS, FROM SPEED TO NEED

the late 1910s to the late 1930s

*Your truck is not so delicate as your watch,
yet its units are machined just as accurately and
its working parts fit just as closely.
Treat it with the consideration that is due a fine
mechanism, and you will be well repaid.*
— Chevrolet truck owner's manual, 1939

It could be argued, without much fear of con-
tradiction, that Chevrolet is best known today
as a manufacturer of trucks. Chevy trucks have
topped their passenger car brethren on the sales
charts for most of the eighties and nineties and,

The 1932 Open Cab Pickup, or Roadster Pickup, is one of
the rarest of all Chevrolet trucks—just 464 were built that
year. The Roadster Pickup was made from 1930 to 1932,
with the 1930 models being the most common—10,444
were built. Sales figures slid to 2,226 in 1931.

Most early Chevrolet trucks were sold new as just a base rolling chassis, engine and cowl, with the appropriate body added later to suit the customer's needs. This 1931 one and one half-ton M-Series truck was fitted with fire truck accouterments by the Luverne Company of Luverne, Minnesota. This truck is the 131in wheelbase model, sold for use in heavier duty applications.

The 1931 six-cylinder was little changed from the powerplant's 1929 introduction. The six's 194ci displacement came from a 3 5/16x3 3/4in bore and stroke. Horsepower was a respectable 50 at 2600rpm.

with the possible exception of the Corvette, the Chevy pickup is easily the most recognizable Chevy product currently made. To most people, the name Chevrolet equals "pickup."

But in the early years of the twentieth century the name "Chevrolet" had far different connotations. Chevrolet meant *speed*, thanks to the high-profile racing careers of Louis, Gaston, and Arthur Chevrolet.

Instruments on 1931 models included a speedometer, odometer, oil pressure gauge, coolant temperature, ammeter and fuel gauge. All of the readouts were located in the center of the dash, rather than in direct view of the driver.

Steel disc wheels first appeared on trucks in 1929, finally replacing wooden spoke wheels. On 1931 models such as this, wheels were 19in in diameter.

Value was the big selling point for Chevy trucks in 1931. Even when bragging about its power, the six-cylinder was pushed as a money-saving feature, offering ". . . valuable time saved on trips to market, and a minimum of costly wear on vital engine parts." Prices listed show half-ton commercial chassis started at $355; one and one half-ton chassis started at $520.

Swiss-born Louis was the best known of the three, with the most far-reaching dreams. Before attaching the family name to what would become the most popular line of cars and trucks in America, Louis worked as a Fiat mechanic, and later turned to auto racing during the early daredevil years of the sport. Louis' fame arose from his exploits on the first Buick racing team, and also his efforts at the early Indianapolis 500 races. The Chevrolet brothers became fixtures at Indianapolis, with Gaston taking the checkered flag at the 1920 Indy 500. Although Gaston died later that year in a racing accident, the surviving brothers became the first team to repeat as Indy 500 winners when Tommy Milton won in 1921 in a Chevrolet-built Frontenac Special.

If Louis had had his way, the Chevrolet division of General Motors might have followed a radically different course. In keeping with his flamboyant image, Louis preferred powerful, well-engineered autos that offered more than just pedestrian transportation. The fact that the Chevrolet division of General Motors is now a maker of working-class cars and trucks can actually be credited more to William Crapo Durant, creator of GM, than to Louis Chevrolet himself.

Durant founded General Motors in 1908, but lost control of the company in 1910 after the fledgling organization piled up substantial

Open Cab Pick-up—Disc wheels standard. Price including body $440. With closed cab $487.50.

It costs less to haul with Chevrolet six-cylinder trucks

One sure way to increase farm profits is to use trucks that *decrease* farm costs. The six-cylinder Chevrolet is built to do exactly that.

A long heavy frame, supported by four long chrome-vanadium springs, allows for a full capacity, Chevrolet-built body. That means bigger loads per trip, fewer trips per job.

Chevrolet's 50-horsepower 6-cylinder engine develops maximum road-speed—smoothly —at a low "r. p. m." That means valuable time saved on trips to market, and a minimum of costly wear on vital engine parts.

Every feature affecting gasoline and oil consumption has been efficiently designed, for higher fuel and oil mileage. The result is fewer stops at the filling station, and lower operating costs.

Axles, frame, clutch, 4-speed transmission and brakes have been made extra-large and

extra-durable. That means *certainty* of performance, every day in the week — less time off for servicing — and a longer-lasting truck.

If you are considering the purchase of hauling equipment, do the really economical thing! Join the thousands of farm owners who are saving money with six-cylinder Chevrolet farm trucks. The new line of Chevrolet-built bodies includes two stakes, two cattle racks, high and wide expresses, and many other body types that are well suited to farm work.

Chevrolet Motor Company
Dept. 20-F, 420 Milwaukee Avenue, West
Detroit, Michigan

Gentlemen—Please send me complete information about Chevrolet's line of six-cylinder trucks with Chevrolet-built bodies.

Name_____

Address_____

City or P. O._____ State_____

1½-Ton 157-Inch Stock Rock Truck—Price complete with Chevrolet cab and body $830. Dual wheels standard. With 131" wheelbase $730, dual wheels $25 extra.

1½-Ton 131-Inch Stake Truck—Price complete with Chevrolet cab and body $710, dual wheels $25 extra. With 157" wheelbase $810, dual wheels standard.

1½-Ton 157-Inch High Wide Express Truck—Price with Chevrolet cab and body $800, dual wheels standard. With 131-inch wheelbase $715, dual wheels $25 extra.

COMMERCIAL CHASSIS **$355**

1½ TON CHASSIS WITH 131-INCH WHEEL-BASE (Dual wheels optional $25 extra) $520
1½-TON CHASSIS WITH 157-INCH WHEEL-BASE (Dual wheels standard) . . . $590

All chassis prices f. o. b. Flint, Michigan. All truck body prices f. o. b. Indianapolis, Indiana. Special equipment extra.

CHEVROLET SIX CYLINDER TRUCKS
FOR LOWEST TRANSPORTATION COST

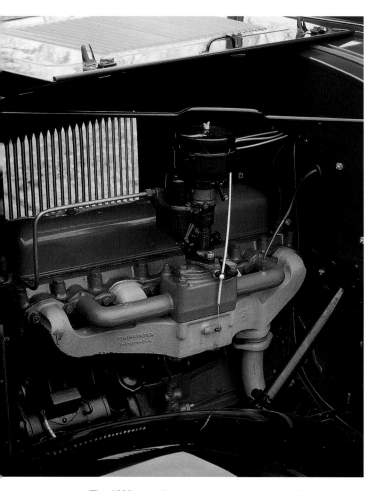

The 1932 six-cylinder engine was upgraded with slightly larger valves, more valve lift from a rocker arm change, a new downdraft carburetor and manifold, a counterbalanced crankshaft and stiffened block. The changes helped bump the 194ci six's horsepower rating to 60 at 3000rpm. The clutch was also revised on 1932 models.

debts. Durant was determined to regain control of the company he had founded, and saw Louis Chevrolet as someone who could help him do it. Durant knew Louis from his days on the Buick racing team, and knew that Louis had aspirations to start his own car company. Durant figured that with his backing he could help get a Chevrolet car company off the ground — which he promptly did.

After financing was secured, Durant set Louis to design the new Chevrolet car. In the meantime, Durant formed the Little Motor Car Company (named after former Buick general manager William Little), to offer a bottom-dollar auto to sell alongside the new Chevrolet. The Little was first out of the gate, in mid-1912. The Chevrolet Model C Classic Six, designed by Louis, arrived later that year.

The two cars perfectly reflected the competing visions of Durant and Chevrolet as to what a viable Chevrolet car should be. Chevrolet's Model C was large and heavy although sturdily designed, was powered by a huge 299ci six-cylinder engine, and was priced at $2,100. Meanwhile, Durant's Little auto was powered by a small four-cylinder, was perhaps somewhat less sturdily designed, and sold for $690. A second Little, the Little Six, was also offered.

Price quickly won out among consumers. The expensive Model C did not sell well; Louis resisted Durant's push for a more economical Chevrolet car. Durant had wanted the Chevrolet car to be considerably smaller and lighter, the better to compete with Ford, and moved to pull the company in that direction. Durant combined Little and Chevrolet in 1913. He dropped the Little name but essentially kept the Little cars, which were incorporated into the Chevrolet line-up.

Cheap, stripped-down cars were not what Louis had in mind, and thus the man who inspired and lent his name to the whole

Although early Chevrolet trucks were initially available in black, and then Blue Bell Blue, most were quickly painted colors appropriate for their new jobs, such as this red 1931 fire truck.

The standard color on Chevy trucks for several years was Blue Bell Blue, as shown here. The Roadster Pickup initially sold for $440, but Chevrolet dropped the prices later in 1932, making the Roadster the lowest priced Chevrolet that year.

Chevrolet enterprise left the company in 1913, not long after the first Chevrolet rolled out the door. Louis worked in a number of other automotive ventures, and he and his brothers had moments in the sun at Indianapolis, but Louis Chevrolet never achieved the personal success that the company bearing his name eventually did.

continued on page 22

The vehicle specification tag was located at the base of the seat on late-twenties models. This 1928 tag, nearly faded to nothingness, shows a chassis weight of 2,030lb and a GVW of 6,150lb, indicating a half-ton AB Series.

Surrounded by a sea of Fords, a lone 1936 Chevrolet (center) makes its way through a Depression-era Texas town. The 1936 half-ton Chevy pickups were the first to receive hydraulic brakes as standard equipment. *Texas Department of Transportation*

Continued from page 19

After a generally positive start with the new Chevrolet company, Durant reacquired General Motors in 1915, largely by swapping shares of Chevrolet stock for GM stock until he had enough to gain control. From then on, with a few missteps, the Chevrolet car was the foot soldier of the General Motors con- glomerate, aimed squarely at the working-class buyer.

Of course, in the rapidly evolving automotive world of the early twentieth century, "working class" transportation soon came to mean more than just a cheap automobile. As cars became more common and more people began to use them in a business capacity, the

Little-changed from its 1937 introduction, the 1939 216ci six cylinder produced 85hp at 3200rpm. The engine arrived at its displacement through a 3 1/2x3 3/4in bore and stroke.

need for a true working vehicle grew. And so the first Chevrolet trucks were born, in 1918.

That first year there were two Chevrolet truck chassis. The first, designated the Model 490 (so named because of the $490 price of the base auto), was a half-ton model based on the Chevrolet passenger car. The second was named the Model T, and was designated a one-ton chassis.

No one was likely to confuse either of these Spartan vehicles with a Cadillac. In fact, the Light Delivery Model 490 half-ton was sold as a semi-finished chassis, without cab or bed—both were to be added by the customer. The truck did come with heavier-duty springs appropriate for carrying heavier loads, but used the same 170.9ci four-cylinder engine as the regular passenger car. Horsepower was listed in the 24-26 range; modest, but in keeping with the competition, and superior to the output of Ford's Model T engine. The Model 490 half-ton Light Delivery chassis sold for a decidedly working-class $595.

The one-ton Model T was considerably more stout. The T used a larger 224ci four-cylinder engine that developed 37hp, and a had worm drive differential. The Model T had a longer wheelbase than the 490, 125in versus 102in, and used larger wheels and tires. The T could also be equipped to look more like a traditional truck, due to the availability of two factory "Express" body types.

Fewer than 1,000 Chevrolet truck chassis were sold in 1918, but production steadily increased, even if the trucks changed little from 1919–1920. By 1920, Chevrolet trucks were an integral part of General Motors. Alas, William C. Durant was not—he had been forced out of

Instrumentation in 1939 included a gas gauge, a speedometer, ammeter, water temperature indicator, and an oil pressure gauge. Regarding the oil pressure gauge, the 1939 owner's manual reminds: "This gauge on the instrument panel is an indicator only, and merely shows whether or not the oil pump is working."

the company a second time for his extravagant business plans. After Durant's departure considerable discussion ensued at GM about Chevrolet's place in the automotive universe, but eventually the decision was made to continue to keep Chevrolet at the lower end of the price spectrum.

In 1921 Chevrolet introduced the three quarter-ton Model G truck chassis, which slotted in between the 490 and Model T in size and price. The Model G had, at 120in, a longer wheelbase

than the Model 490, a heavier-duty frame, and larger wheels and tires, although it used the same 170.9ci engine as the 490. Although an indicator of things to come, the Model G had a short life, and was phased out at the end of 1922.

The Model 490 and Model T lasted until their replacements, the Series B and D trucks, were introduced in 1923. As before, the B was a light-duty half-ton truck based on passenger car mechanicals, while the D was a heavier, one-ton vehicle. The changes in the truck line reflected the new styling and features on the 1923 Chevrolet passenger cars. One of the most noticeable was a higher hoodline. The half-ton also benefited from more power, with the 170.9ci four-cylinder churning out 35hp at 1900rpm. The one-ton was switched to a 120in wheelbase from the previous year's 125in.

The model designations changed again in 1924, even if the trucks themselves did not. Called Series F and H, the two were essentially the same as the previous year's Series B and D. In fact, model name changes were a yearly event in the twenties, even if significant upgrades came a little more sparingly. The four-cylinder engine and clutch were redesigned for greater strength and easier service in 1925. All-steel bodies were available on one-ton trucks by 1926, and a Sedan Delivery model was added in 1928.

By the late 1920s, Chevrolet was selling more than 100,000 truck chassis a year, and gaining fast on Henry Ford's Model T. When Ford shut down Model T production in 1927 to retool for the Model A, Chevrolet truck sales slipped past Ford for the first time, beginning a see-saw battle for market domination that has waged for decades.

For its part, Chevrolet waged the battle for sales in the late 1920s with a series of noteworthy improvements, such as the introduction of four-wheel brakes and expanded choice of body styles in 1928. The most important positive change came the following year, when the 1929 trucks were introduced with a new, overhead valve, 194ci six-cylinder engine as standard equipment. The 46hp six helped push the Chevrolet past the four-cylinder Model A Ford, literally and figuratively, while maintaining prices at the entry level end of the market.

Variations of the six-cylinder became a mainstay of the Chevrolet truck line, surviving well into the 1950s. The overhead valve design was relatively advanced for the time, and with good reason became a bragging point in Chevrolet's early ads. The six's 46hp output was greater than that of Ford's Model A four-cylinder at 40hp, as well as other competitors' engines.

The 1930s saw much more rapid change in the truck market in general, and at Chevrolet in particular. Body styles were changed more frequently, and mechanical advances were incorporated on a more regular basis. This was due partly to rapid technological change, partly to the distinct design trends of the thirties, and partly to the unstable market conditions of the Great Depression.

For 1930 the six-cylinder's horsepower was increased to 50, and an electric gas gauge was added. In 1931 Chevrolet began offering a choice of colors, instead of just black, as was the case through 1928, and blue, which was the standard color from 1929 to 1930. Also in 1931, Chevrolet started offering "factory" truck bodies, after the purchase of the Martin-Parry company, a supplier of truck bodies. In 1932, Chevrolet cars received their own new sheetmetal, while the trucks kept the look shared by both in 1931. The different look between the two was an indicator of things to come. In 1934 Chevrolet car and truck styling diverged completely, with the truck line getting its own sheetmetal.

Horsepower continued to inch up; by 1932 it was up to 60hp, and by 1933 it was up to 65 after the six was stroked to 206.5ci. Power went up to 80 in 1935, thanks largely to a bump in compression ratio and a new cylinder head. To handle the increasing horsepower, hydraulic brakes were mercifully incorporated into Chevy trucks in 1936. Ford trucks would not share this innovation until 1939.

One of the most thorough restyles of the Chevy truck line came in 1937. With its more

streamlined cab, rounded nose and more decorative grille, the '37 models moved even further away from the simple, stripped down looks so common on 1920s trucks. The six cylinder was substantially revised that year as well, displacing 216.5ci and 85hp.

Through the late thirties and early forties, changes in the light duty Chevy truck line were mostly limited to slight body and trim variations, plus some improvements to the interior, right up until the new 1941 models launched on the eve of World War II. By December 1941, events in Europe and the Pacific forced plenty of changes in the company. As with so many areas of endeavor in the twentieth century, the American auto industry's history is usually divided into pre-war and post-war eras. The war remains a sort of demarcation line, with styling and engineering from the two eras as distinct as night and day.

But along with the end of the Great Depression and the beginning of World War II, there was another marker of the passing of an era. Louis Chevrolet—racer, designer, entrepreneur and namesake of the most popular cars and trucks in America—died in 1941. He died in relative obscurity, but the vehicles bearing his name achieved a fame few could surpass.

2

POSTWAR AND PRIME TIME

the mid 1940s to the late 1950s

With the nation genuinely at risk from foreign invaders for the first time since the War of 1812, the federal government ordered a shutdown of civilian car and truck production on February 9, 1942. For the next three years, virtually all auto industry production capacity was converted to the manufacture of the implements of war. The mighty General Motors empire was a key player in the creation of the armaments necessary to crush Hitler's armies and Imperial Japan's expansionist dreams. Cadillac made tanks, Chevrolet made military trucks, Pontiac made anti-aircraft cannons, Buick made shell casings; an astonishing number of the machines used to fight the Germans and the Japanese came from GM factories.

As this 1949 3100 model illustrates, the post-war Advance Design Series incorporated more glass area and a larger cab than the prewar designs. The chrome grille was part of the DeLuxe trim package. The Advance Design Series is a good example of how all the automakers moved toward cleaner design after WWII. This series was the last to use the split windshield.

Interior dimensions of the Advance Design trucks were wider and longer than the early 1947 models. Deluxe Cab models benefited from greater visibility thanks to additional rear quarter windows. Optional radios were becoming slightly more common, but were still a rare sight in pickups.

With so much effort devoted to wartime production, at war's end all GM — or any of the country's automakers — had to offer was a collection of 1942 leftovers. The "new" 1946 civilian Chevy pickups were identical in almost every way to the 1942 models; same styling, same 216.5ci six-cylinder with 90hp, same suspension. They were still available in half-ton and three quarter-ton designations, although

the one ton was added back to the line-up, along with a one-ton "dooley."

The first "all-new" postwar Chevrolets were the "Advance Design" models, put into production in mid-1947. The new Chevy trucks were a clear departure from the previous models, with styling that included a more rounded cab, headlamps nearly flush with the fenders, and a modern hood design — modern in the sense that the hood opened from the front and was hinged at the rear, with no hood side panels for the first time. Also gone after what seemed a lifetime of use was the crank-open windshield.

The main impression left by the Advance Design Series was a move toward cleaner styling. The new horizontal five-bar grille was a much simpler design than the busy grille of the previous truck. The interior was also redesigned, with the cab dimensions enlarged and more glass area than

Engine monitoring gauges were featured in a cluster to the left of the steering column, the speedometer to the right. The speedometer read to 100mph on the 1946 and early 1947 trucks, but backtracked a bit on the Advance Design series.

This beautiful 1949 half-ton has factory radio and bias ply tires. It was restored by its owners, Rodney Bergum and Bill Webster; proof that outstanding work can come out of the home shops of amateurs. They did all of the work themselves, except for the chrome-plating and upholstery. *Tom Brownell collection*

previously. The bed was enlarged to increase cargo capacity.

Mechanically, though, there was much that was familiar on the new trucks. The engine was still the venerable 216ci six, the transmission choices were familiar three-speed and four-speed units, and the frame, though strengthened, was essentially the same design. The new models were designated 3100 for half-ton, 3600 for three quarter-ton, and 3800 for one-ton. The trucks were available in the usual variety of configurations, including Canopy Express, Panel Truck, Stake Bed and Suburban. Half-ton pickup prices started at $1,087.

Even though Chevy, Ford and Dodge all introduced their new postwar trucks within a year of each other, all sold well, especially the Chevy. Truck sales topped a quarter million for the 1947 calendar year, tens of thousands more than the year before.

Also still alive during this time was the perennial sedan delivery vehicle. Based on passenger car mechanicals, the sedan delivery was essentially a station wagon with the rear and side glass areas given over to sheetmetal. Many of these cars were used as trucks in a variety of occupations. The first new postwar Chevrolet Sedan Deliveries were introduced for 1949. Like

Wooden bed floors were still in use in 1949 trucks. Bed length was 78in, while width stretched to 50in.

The Deluxe cab included rear quarter windows on the cab. The rear bumper was an optional piece of equipment. Half-ton pickup prices started at $1,253 in 1949.

the 1948 trucks, the '49 Deliveries were blessed with a more streamlined shape than the earlier models, and were a bit larger. Sedan Delivery annual production usually ranged between 8,000 to 20,000 through most of the fifties.

The basic body style of the Advance Design Series trucks continued until mid-1955, with a

If you could pinpoint the era when Chevy trucks became more than just farm vehicles, you'd zero in on the 1950s. With their upscale trim, unique bed, and comfort options, the Cameo Carriers of 1955-1958 (1956 shown) were perfect for stepping out on the town, but were still plenty capable of hauling manure if you really had to.

few improvements along the way. A larger, 235ci "Loadmaster" six-cylinder was added to the line-up in 1950, available on some heavier duty models. A Suburban Carryall with regular doors at the rear instead of a tailgate was also added that year. Push-button door handles were added in 1952. A 235ci six replaced the 216 in light-duty trucks in 1953. And the 1954 models received a much more pronounced nose treatment, a look that only lasted until mid-1955, when the new "Second Series" trucks were introduced — to near universal acclaim.

The 1955-1957 Chevrolet cars and trucks are arguably the most popular Chevrolets of all time. Later models sometimes sold in greater numbers, but few Chevrolets have achieved the lasting fame and owner appreciation as those breakthrough designs. The popular attraction to these models comes from more than just surface appeal, but the styling of the 1955 Chevrolet cars and trucks captured a look that has proven to be one of the most enduring American design statements this century.

The cars featured clean, well-proportioned styling, with smooth bodysides replacing the pontooned fenders of previous years, and a minimum (for the time) of chrome. The trucks shared in this move toward visual restraint, with fenders and hood seeming less separate parts and more an integrated assembly. The grille was a functional-looking egg-crate design and, like the cars, the trucks were conservatively adorned with chrome, emblems and the like. Buyers had a choice of a short box pickup, built on the

HELCK

Nicely illustrated ads from the late forties and early fifties depicted Chevy trucks in all types of hard-working situations. Prices for half-ton pickups started at $1,407 in 1953, less for just the chassis and cab.

How Chevrolet trucks are engineered and powered to handle heavy loads over rough roads . . .

The crushing weight of mammoth logs tests the stamina and power of any truck. It is final proof of qualities carefully "engineered in." And a truck that handles such tremendous loads yet retains efficiency and easy handling characteristics is a truck to depend on for *any* kind of job.

Chevrolet for 1953 is such a truck. Typical of its fine engineering is the splined rear axle to hub connection on heavy-duty models. Driving splines mate directly with wheel hubs to distribute stress evenly, eliminate loose axle shaft bolts and grease leaks. This is just one example of how every Chevrolet truck is factory-matched to the job. And in 1953 Chevrolet has even greater heavy-duty power than before.

Already thousands of satisfied users have discovered Chevrolet trucks are engineered for new dependability, new ruggedness and for even greater over-all economy in 1953.

Best of all, they list for less than any other trucks of comparable capacity and specifications.

Let your Chevrolet dealer show you how much more you get with Chevrolet trucks—*and how much less you need pay!* Chevrolet Division of General Motors, Detroit 2, Michigan.

RIGHT
The 1956 Cameo Carrier differed little from the 1955 models. Changes included additional color options. After a big first year in 1955, Cameo sales dropped to only 1,452 in 1956.

114in wheelbase, and a long box pickup, built on a 123 1/4in wheelbase.

Of course, the new truck's sheetmetal may have been clean and uncluttered, but that didn't mean it wasn't stylish. Many of the '55's styling features were quite eye-catching at the time, such as the wraparound windshield. And if a buyer was looking for a truly stylish truck, there was the special tricked-out and suited-up Cameo Carrier model — essentially a "factory custom" truck with several car-like features and styling touches not normally found on pickups.

The Cameo Carrier featured flush, fiberglass bed sides that mimicked the cab's body lines, with a simple chrome strip separating the bed from the cab. And that cab had a dramatic rear window that stretched from one end of the cab to the other. The taillights were unique to the Cameo, full wheel covers were added, and

An AM radio was optional on Chevy trucks in 1956. With its Chevy Bowtie emblem and oval shape, the radio was well-integrated into the Chevy's handsome dash.

The Cameo interior continued the two-tone theme. The upper dash, steering wheel and floor mat mimicked the outer cab's Cardinal Red trim. The bed was also painted to match the accenting color.

the grille and bumpers were chromed to further dress up Chevy's flashiest new pickup. The Cameo was available in one only color combination in 1955, Bombay Ivory with Cardinal Red trim. Other colors were added in later years.

As could be expected, Cameos were substantially more expensive than regular stepside

Before Chevrolet added four-wheel drive to its option list in 1957, most Chevy trucks relied on NAPCO four-wheel drive components, like this 1955 Carryall Suburban. NAPCO, based out of Minneapolis, Minnesota, performed the conversions at their shop, or the modifications could be performed at Chevrolet or GMC dealers. Carryall Suburbans were available with either ambulance-style doors in the rear or a traditional pickup-type tailgate. *Jim Knight, "Pickups 'n Panels in Print"*

The 1954 pickups returned to the one-piece windshield design of earlier models. The '54's prominent grille had a short life, lasting only until mid-'55, after which the "second series" 1955s were introduced. A bragging point in advertisements like this was Chevy's new optional Hydra-Matic automatic transmission.

Your savings start early and never stop with new Chevrolet trucks!

In fact, your savings start even before you start the engine of your new Chevrolet truck. As soon as you close the deal, you're money ahead. The reason, of course, is that Chevrolet is America's lowest-priced line of trucks. But that's only one of the many money-saving advantages you'll enjoy with a new Chevrolet truck.

For example, you'll save plenty on operating costs. Thanks to new high-compression engine performance, you get increased power *plus* money-saving gas mileage in every model.

You'll save on upkeep costs, too. That's because these great new Chevrolet trucks have extra strength and stamina built into vital chassis units.

And when it comes time to trade your Chevrolet truck in on a new one, you save again. Chevrolet, you know, is the truck with a traditionally higher trade-in value.

Why not visit your Chevrolet dealer soon and find out how easy it is to start saving with a new Chevrolet truck. . . . Chevrolet Division of General Motors, Detroit 2, Michigan.

New Chevrolet trucks offer more advantages you need and want—

New Engine Power: Brawnier "Thriftmaster 235" engine. Rugged "Loadmaster 235." All-new "Jobmaster 261" engine.*

New Comfortmaster Cab: Offers new comfort, safety and convenience. New one-piece curved windshield provides extra visibility.

New Chassis Ruggedness: Heavier axle shafts in 2-ton models . . . newly designed clutches, and more rigid frames in *all* models.

New Ride Control Seat*: Seat cushion and back move as a unit to eliminate back-rubbing. It "floats" you over rough roads with ease.

New Automatic Transmission*: Proved truck Hydra-Matic transmission is offered on ½-, ¾- and 1-ton models.

New, Bigger Load Space: New pickup bodies have deeper sides. New stake and platform bodies are wider, longer and roomier.

Optional at extra cost. Ride Control Seat is available in standard cabs only, "Jobmaster 261" engine on 2-ton models.

CHEVROLET TRUCKS
Most Trustworthy Trucks on Any Job!

first in demand in value in sales   CHEVROLET

The Cameo's bed sides and tailgate were fiberglass. The taillights and rear bumper were specific to the Cameo; the center section opens to reveal the spare tire carrier.

pickups, with prices starting nearly $500 higher than that of the base pickup, and the fancy trucks could easily be optioned up to nearly $3,300. Still, 5,220 Cameos found buyers that first year, the best year of the Cameo's four-year production run.

But it wasn't just styling that made the 1955 trucks a hit. Under the skin was one major technical advance, a new lightweight, overhead valve, high-revving V-8 engine. The 265ci small-block V-8 was Chevy's first V-8 since the obscure 286ci V-8 of 1917 and 1918. While the WWI-era V-8 used dual carburetors, exhaust manifolds formed inside the cylinder heads, and produced a whopping 55hp, the new V-8 took advantage of decades of research into engine development by other GM divisions.

If there was a job to do, there was an appropriate truck to get it done. This 1955 panel truck was specially modified for "nail picking." The unusual rear fender flares house dual rear wheels, not normally available on panel trucks and Suburbans. *Texas Department of Transportation*

With the engine program spearheaded by Ed Cole, Chevrolet's chief engineer, the new V-8's development team made light weight, compact dimensions and simplicity their design goals — goals they achieved in spectacular fashion. The finished V-8 engine weighed less than the company's six-cylinder power-plant, and was physically more compact than virtually every other V-8 in existence. The efficient end product came thanks to a compact engine block with short side skirts that ended just below the centerline of the crankshaft, and cylinder heads pared to the lightest weight and smallest size possible.

Chevy trucks were fitted with all manner of gear for unusual jobs. This 1957 pickup is equipped with a traffic cone picker, ideal for speeding up the job. *Texas Department of Transportation*

Extremely handsome trucks by any standards, these were still considered working trucks, as this picture shows. Clyde Horst's 1956 Stepside has the optional exterior sun visor. *Roy Query, courtesy* Automobile Quarterly

Besides economical dimensions, the small-block offered good performance potential. The low reciprocating mass of the small-block made it a quick revving engine, and the wedge-shaped combustion chambers, in-line valve configuration and inexpensive, lightweight valvetrain helped make the engine a favorite of performance buffs. The

The 1957 Cameo incorporated several styling changes over the previous two years. The chrome grille put forward a much more stylized face than the egg-crate '55 and '56 models, as did the zoomy new hood ornaments. A "V" badge on the doors identified the truck as a V-8 model. The new trim and stripe down the bedside offered Cameo identification.

1955 265ci V-8 had a compression ratio of 7.5:1, breathed through a two-barrel carburetor and used a 12-volt electrical system. The truck version of the engine was rated at 145hp, and was called the "Trademaster" engine. Some form of that original 265ci V-8 has been available in every full-size Chevy pickup built since then.

Naturally, the GMC truck line-up changed in 1955 right along with the Chevy. The basic body lines of the GMC were identical to those of the Chevy, although the GMC grille and front-end treatment were much more stylized than the uncomplicated Chevy front end. The GMC did not share the new small-block 265ci V-8, but GMC trucks did get Pontiac's 287ci V-8 underhood, which at the time was even more powerful than the new Chevy V-8.

The Cameo was actually identified as such in 1957, thanks to emblems affixed to the front of the bed.

The 1957 Chevrolet trucks came standard with painted grille and bumper, but chrome pieces were optional. Indian Turquoise was one of the many new colors offered for 1957. The "V" emblems on the doors indicate this original, unrestored truck houses the 265ci V-8 underhood. *Jim Knight, "Pickups 'n Panels in Print"*

With so much changed for 1955, the following year's Chevy trucks strayed little from
the new blueprint. The exterior trim was
moved around a bit and some new colors were
added, along with some extra horsepower for
both the Thriftmaster 235 six and Trademaster
265 V-8. A new grille arrived for 1957, and
the large rear window became standard on all
light duty pickups, but otherwise, change was
minimal. Chevrolet did begin offering facto-
ry-available four-wheel drive in 1957,

The 1957 pickups maintained the V-shaped instrument
cluster introduced in 1955. The Cameo continued to use
the two-tone paint scheme.

Cameo interior niceties included partially upholstered
door panels that matched the seat coverings.

though. Prior to that (and after) NAPCO 4x4
conversion kits were the norm for Chevrolet
off-roaders.

But the car and truck markets were noth-
ing if not dynamic in the 1950s. Chevrolet's
relative styling stability lasted only until 1958,
when a new body style with quad headlamps, a
new grille, and a new "fleet side" body with a
wider bed and flush bed sides was introduced.
Along with the new look in light-duty trucks
was a new name, "Apache." Under the skin, the
265ci V-8's displacement was increased to 283
cubic inches, and the factory-offered four-
wheel drive system was available across the
model range, including in Suburbans. The
Cameo Carrier took its last bow in 1958, with
only 1,405 built.

The big news for 1959 was the introduction
of the car/truck hybrid El Camino. The El Camino

All Cameo Carriers used the large wraparound rear window. Cameo sales rose slightly in 1957 from year-earlier totals, to 2,244 units. The price of the fancy truck was still a hindrance to high-volume sales.

was built in response to Ford's Ranchero, another truck made from car underpinnings, which was introduced for 1957. The novelty and success of the Ranchero caught GM off-guard, and represented one of the few times Chevrolet was caught with its corporate pants around its ankles by Ford.

The El Camino used passenger car chassis and suspension, which in 1959 meant a boxed X-frame, a 119in wheelbase, 1,150lb load capacity, and unequal length control arms with coil springs for the front suspension. The truck also used coil springs in the rear. The El Camino's overall length was 211in, making it longer than Chevrolet's base Apache full-size pickup, and heavier, too. Naturally, the 1959 Sedan Delivery also adopted the radical new passenger car styling.

Since the El Camino was based on the Chevy passenger car, it was available with a full

Whereas the Cameo Carrier had Chevy's small-block V-8 as an option, GMC's 1957 Suburban used a 347ci Pontiac engine, rated at 206hp. The 1955 and 1956 models used smaller Pontiac V-8 engines. Like the Cameo, the Suburban was offered from 1955-1958. Pinstripes on this '57 are owner additions.

GMC trucks were usually better equipped than their Chevrolet counterparts, and often contained such luxuries as GM's Hydra-Matic automatic transmission. Base price for a Suburban pickup was $2,498, about $200 higher than a Cameo Carrier.

range of passenger car engines, unlike the rest of the truck line. El Camino engines included a 235ci six, a 283ci V-8 with two-barrel carburetor, and a 283 four-barrel. Even the fuel-injected 283 was listed in factory literature. The 348ci W-head V-8 introduced in 1958 was also available in the El Camino, in four-barrel (250hp), and triple two-barrel guise (280hp), plus special 300hp and 315hp high-compression versions of the four- and six-barrel engines.

Although earlier prewar trucks had also been built off passenger car mechanicals, and the Cameo Carrier had the extra flash, the El Camino was Chevrolet's first true high-performance pickup.

Road testers of the time were smitten with the El Camino's power, although they

The 1958 models received quad headlamps, a busier grille, and the Apache designation. The wider, slab-sided Fleetside bed was introduced for 1958, but the Stepside bed was still the price leader. The 1959 models were almost identical, although the Chevrolet Apache emblem was redesigned and moved farther forward on the fender. *Jim Knight, "Pickups 'n Panels in Print"*

The one-ton platform models rode on a 135in wheelbase in 1957, as compared to the 123in and 114in wheelbases of the smaller trucks. Prices started at $2,274.

Ads from 1958 touted the new Fleetside's good looks, but made sure to emphasize the truck's tough features, such as "double-walled lower body construction," and "husky parallel-design frame." The 1958 Fleetside cost only slightly more than the stepside pickup. A recession that year hurt truck sales across the board.

were a bit less enthusiastic about the truck's handling. "When empty, the El Camino will handle very well although the slow ratio of the standard steering will keep a driver plenty busy on a twisting mountain road," said *Hot Rod's* Ray Brock in a February 1959 road test of a 315hp Camino. "The soft springing will allow the El Camino to lean in an alarming manner on corners but after reaching a heeled-over position, the El Camino will get a good grip on the road and go through the corners with good control and feel." With the 315hp, triple-car-bureted 348ci engine, four-speed transmission and 3.36 axle ratio, *Hot Rod* clocked the El Camino at 16.0 seconds at 90mph through the

New! The Handsomest, Hardest Working Farm Hand On Four Wheels!

It's Chevrolet's new Fleetside pickup. It combines new style and load space with stamina and economy that are typical of every truck in the Task-Force 58 lineup!

Take a good look at the best looking pickup of all —Chevrolet's new Fleetside! Here's a truck capable of fitting into almost any farm chore you've got—from hauling stones to hauling groceries. Like all Chevies, it's styled for your pride, engineered for work. Like all Chevies, it's built for *big loads*—its body is a full 6 feet wide, and is available in lengths of 78″ and 98″. *You get the greatest load space of any comparable low-priced pickup!* Double-walled lower body construction adds extra strength to the cargo box. Loading heights are low and the gastight tailgate becomes a sturdy platform for extra-long loads when extended.

Powerful short-stroke V8 engines offer stamina and performance that are hard to beat. And improved 6's get the most out of a gallon of gas—keep costs down, down, *down!* Husky parallel-design frame totes king-sized loads without strain, sturdy axles and spring suspensions protect cargos, add long life, offer around-the-clock economy. There's hustle, muscle and style in *every* Chevy. Ask your Chevrolet dealer to show you the right truck for your farm job. See him today. . . . Chevrolet Division of General Motors, Detroit 2, Michigan.

CHEVROLET
TASK·FORCE 58 CHEVROLET TRUCKS

The passenger car-based El Camino made its debut for 1959. Although more car than truck, the El Camino had a double-wall pickup bed and a load capacity of 1,200lb when optioned with oversize tires and heavy-duty springs. The example pictured has an owner-installed bed cover. *Jim Knight, "Pickups 'n Panels in Print"*

This three quarter-ton Stepside pickup was one of very few built in 1959. The Stepside was available in box lengths of 6.5ft, 8ft, and 9ft. The '59 36 Series shown here has the shortest box available, the standard painted front bumper, and rear-wheel drive. Chrome bumpers were an option, as was four-wheel drive for the 36 Series. *GM Photographic/Golden State Pickup Parts Archive*

quarter mile. Good numbers, and Brock noted how much potential was still available. "With a gear ratio of about 4.55 to 1 and the optional positraction differential, this car would break 100mph in the quarter and come close to 14 seconds flat."

This 1959 half-ton Fleetside Apache 32 is as deluxe as they come: 98in body, Flight-Ride cab with Panoramic windshield, optional Torque-Action brakes, chrome moldings, and new color combinations. *GM Photographic/Golden State Pickup Parts Archive*

The styling of the 1958 Cameo changed once again, switching to quad headlamps and an even busier grille than before. Pinstripes are owner additions.

The regular light-duty Chevy Apache pickup was mostly unchanged for 1959 except for trim variations. But the '59s fittingly wrapped up the decade as the last models of the body style so readily identified with that time period. The 1960 trucks debuted with the square lines that would quickly become associated with cars and trucks of that decade. But few vehicles captured the flavor of their times better than the Chevy trucks of the 1950s.

3

SQUARE TRUCKS IN A MOD AGE

the 1960s to the early 1970s

In 1960 Chevrolet trucks took another distinct styling turn. But even more so than in the 1950s, the definition of what constituted a Chevrolet truck was being expanded to include a fascinating array of vehicles in the 1960s — and it wasn't just styling or packaging leading the way, but technical innovation as well.

Many of those innovations trickled into the product mix throughout the decade. Initially though, for 1960, the line-up of light-duty trucks still consisted of half-ton, three quarter-ton and

Truck styling trends in the sixties tended toward the square. The rounded lines of the forties and fifties were left behind as all Chevy trucks, from El Camino to Corvair to C-10, adopted the crisply folded lines popular at the time. Shown is a 1968 C-10, a vintage fast becoming popular with collectors.

The square look of the sixties was launched with the 1960 models. The 1961 models, as shown here in Apache 10 garb, differ mostly just in the grille and trim from the 1960 models. Engine choices included the 235ci and 261ci six, plus the 283ci V-8.

one-ton trucks, a Sedan Delivery, Carryall Suburban and the El Camino. The pickup's new look was the big news. The '60 models debuted with the square silhouette that would dominate domestic truck styling for most of the next three decades. After decades of brawny, bulging-fendered truck styling, the fenders were finally pulled in under the outer edges of the hood and cab.

The body shape was simple and block-like, although the front end was still highly stylized. Two ovoid pods at the leading edge of the hood contained parking lamp assemblies, with a large Chevy Bow Tie emblem between them, at the front of a sunken

year, half-ton pickups were identified as C-10 models, three quarter-tons were called C-20, and one-tons were named C-30. Four-wheel drive trucks were identified with a "K" designation in place of the "C," although they had no external K markings until later years. The trucks received a new Torsion Bar independent front suspension, another harbinger of things to come in the pickup market. Engine choices were still the 235 six and 283 V-8.

The El Camino returned for 1960, with its styling cleaned up somewhat, although the "bat wings" remained. Chevy's car-based truck was discontinued after 1960 though, as the company maintained the 1961 body styles were incompatible with the truck conversion concept. The El Camino returned in 1964, patterned after Ford's smaller, Falcon-based Ranchero. In the case of the Chevy, the smaller donor platform was the new Malibu.

But Chevrolet wasn't the only GM division with truck news for 1960. GMC also introduced its new truck, with all the design changes of the

Instrumentation on Corvair trucks was minimal. Interior options included a radio, gasoline or direct-air heater and defroster, choice of bench or right-hand single seat, and two-speed wipers.

center section of the hood. The Deluxe models still used substantial amounts of chrome in the grille, and the quad headlamps were still en vogue.

Besides the ageless three-block design, the 1960 trucks introduced model designations that have survived into the present. Starting that

RIGHT
The Corvair 95 Rampside pickup featured a unique side-mounted gate that dropped open to form a loading ramp. The side gate worked to the Corvair's advantage, since the truck's rear engine configuration meant a greater lift-over height when loading from the tailgate. The Rampside was produced from 1961-1964. This Corvair truck has been custom-painted by the owner.

Chevy, but also with a new 305ci V-6 under hood. The 305 put out 142hp and 260lb-ft of torque, splitting the difference between the standard Chevy 235ci six and the optional 283ci V-8. The V-6 was an unusual engine configuration in 1960, ahead of its time in some respects. Three decades later, V-6s were standard equipment on just about every full-size truck.

One of the novel Chevrolet trucks of the early '60s was built not in response to

continued on page 66

Corvair Rampside prices started at $2,133 in 1961, slightly more than a base half-ton pickup. The Series 95's air-cooled, aluminum-block six was known for leaking and blowing oil, and the unusual pickup never quite caught on with the public.

62

Deciphering the Code

Chevrolet trucks have had more model names, designations, and advertising nicknames over the years than some competitors' trucks have had nuts and bolts. In early years Chevy trucks carried little, if any external badging, but the postwar models carried a bewildering variety of emblems boasting a veritable alphanumeric soup. This is a partial guide to deciphering some of the Chevy truck numerology.

The 3100 designation was the base half-ton pickup's call letters from 1947-1959. Three quarter-ton trucks were labeled 3600.

The 3800 emblem meant the viewer was looking at a one-ton truck. The 3800 designation shadowed the 3100 and 3600 lifespan, from 1947 to 1959.

Although internally designated the 3124 from 1955-1958, the Cameo Carrier only wore 3124 external badging in 1957.

The original Chevy Bowtie design sprang from William Crapo Durant's fertile mind. The accepted story is that he first saw the design on hotel room wallpaper, and decided to use it as the Chevrolet logo. It first appeared as early as 1913. Shown is a 1928 truck.

The Corvair 95 tag was affixed to commercial versions of the Corvair line, such as the Rampside and Loadside pickups and the Corvan vans. The "95" stood for the 95in wheelbase on which these vehicles were based.

The C-10 designation has been the code for the base half-ton pickup from 1960 to the present day. Three quarter-ton trucks are labeled C-20, while one-ton trucks are tagged C-30. Four-wheel drive models receive a "K" designation in place of the C.

The SS396 emblem indicated high performance, and lots of it. All the go-fast goodies the Chevelle inherited were available on the El Camino. Standard SS396 equipment included a special heavy-duty suspension, domed hood, special instrumentation and that thumping 350hp engine.

The Cheyenne Super equipment helped transform a basic work truck into a higher-profile, comfortable cruiser. The Cheyenne option was introduced in 1971.

In most ways the Corvair-based trucks were a completely different animal from the more conventional pickups, right down to insignia. Judging by sales numbers, most consumers found the species too alien. The best year for the Rampside pickup was the first year, 1961, when 10,787 were sold.

Equipped with mag wheels and other performance modifications, the mid-sixties Chevy trucks make fine street machines. With the availability of ever larger V-8 engines in the sixties, making a Chevy truck into a hot rod was considerably easier than in the fifties. The '65 shown here carries a 427 between its fenders.

Continued from page 62

competition from traditional rivals Ford, Dodge, International or Studebaker, although they played a part, but in reaction to the popularity of Germany's Volkswagen. The Volkswagen van had made great sales inroads in the U.S., and the success of the upstart European import had not gone unnoticed by the Big Three American automakers. Thus Ford introduced the Econoline Van in 1961, Dodge debuted their

"If there's something that needs to be done, it can be done with a pickup." In this case, carrying signs is the task. Although Chevy trucks had slowly become more comfortable and better looking, base work trucks such as this '63 still looked the part, with painted bumpers and dog-dish hubcaps. The base Fleetside six-cylinder pickup cost $2,025 in 1963. *Texas Department of Transportation*

A100 series in 1964, and Chevrolet trotted out the Corvair Van in 1961. All three also offered forward-control pickup versions of their new vans, but Chevrolet did them one better, technologically speaking, with their Corvair 95 Rampside Pickup.

Like the Corvair auto, the vans and pickups used a rear-mounted, air-cooled, horizontally opposed six-cylinder engine. The "flat six" displaced 145ci and produced 80hp and 128lb-ft of torque. It was a novel approach in pickup design, but not without its drawbacks. Since the engine was rear-mounted, it created a protrusion into the rear cargo area. The solution was the "Rampside" version of the Corvair 95, with a unique side-mounted loading door that opened to form a loading ramp into the center of the vehicle.

The Corvair vans and trucks were just part of the expanding array of light-duty commercial vehicles becoming available in the sixties. Another Chevrolet contribution was the more conventional Chevyvan, introduced in 1964. The Chevyvan had the traditional front

Even adorned with aftermarket performance equipment, the 1965 interior's logical, functional design shines through. Beside performance, mid-sixties trucks offered more comfort and convenience items as well.

engine, rear drive configuration of most American vehicles. But it too was geared toward economy, with a 153ci four-cylinder as the sole powerplant. At 167in and slightly more than 2,700lbs, it cut a remarkable svelte path across the country's highways, especially compared to the type of oversize vehicles associated with the fifties.

The traditional C/K-Series pickups enjoyed relative styling stability through the early- to mid-sixties, and Chevy was able to maintain its sales lead over Ford. Most of the external

changes to these models involved different grilles or trim variations from year to year, with the overall trend toward cleaner styling.

Styling changes may have been more frequent in the 1950s, but that doesn't mean the major automakers had grown complacent. In the sixties, the battle for truck supremacy was waged in large part under the hood. Whereas once a single six-cylinder could power an entire truck line for decades, in the sixties each manufacturer tried to leapfrog the other in displacement and power ratings—just as was happening

A working classic

Cast an eye on a rare collector's item. El Camino. Takes on half-ton loads with a hefty frame and a six-and-a-half-foot-long cargo box. Takes it easy on standard Superlift air-adjustable rear shock absorbers. And there's a Positraction rear axle available for holding down spins. So load up. And load on the goodies. Like Strato-bucket seats, air conditioning, tach . . . the works. Everything goes with El Camino's snappy standard or custom interior. El Camino goes with more than 60 power-train combinations. Order from two

Six and five V8 engines up to 350 horses. Match up your power plant with one of five manual and two automatic transmissions. Then put some teeth into your combo with the right axle ratio. For the right safety features, check El Camino's new set of standards: GM-developed energy-absorbing steering column, four-way hazard warning flasher, dual master-cylinder brake system and many more. Get a load of El Camino at your Chevy dealer's. . . . Chevrolet Division of General Motors, Detroit, Michigan.

El Camino

Rear air shocks were standard equipment on the 1967 El Camino. Another bragging point was that more than sixty powertrain combinations were available, the benefit of being based on the mid-size Chevelle platform.

in the passenger car segment of the market. At Chevrolet, the escalation started with the installation into the truck line-up of the optional 327ci V-8 in light duty trucks in 1965 and 1966. The 327 had a 9.25:1 compression ratio, and was rated at 220hp.

The addition of the larger 327 V-8 was definitely part of an industry-wide trend. Ford's truck V-8 engines had been upgraded from the Y-block 292ci in the early '60s to the big-block 352ci in 1965. Dodge was also in the V-8 game, starting the decade with a 318ci V-8 optional, and later throwing a 426ci brute into the mix in a Custom Sports Package. Late in the decade a 383ci big-block was Dodge's optional engine. Even Chevy's six-cylinders were being beefed

Relatively few buyers ordered the 115in wheelbase shortbed Fleetside C-10 in 1968, but it made for a handsome package. Nearly five times as many buyers opted for the 127in wheelbase longbed Fleetside, a more logical choice for most work situations. (The shortbed was more popular among stepside and 4x4 buyers, however.)

Accessory hubcaps in 1968 utilized non-functional lug nuts for that oh-so functional look. The owner reports that, yes, inattentive service station attendants have tried to zap them off with an air ratchet.

Federal safety mandates were making themselves known in the truck world, with front and rear side marker lamps required for 1968. The 250ci six remained the base engine.

The base interior featured a clean, functional appearance. Three-on-the-tree shifter was still standard equipment.

up, with the introduction of the "high torque" 230ci and 292ci engines in 1963.

Chevrolet's big-block engine arrived between truck fenders in 1968. First introduced in the 1965 Corvette, Malibu SS and other car models, the 396ci V-8 had a 4.09x3.76 bore and stroke, featured staggered valves and fantastic "breathing" ability. In pickup form it had a 9.0:1 compression ratio, four-barrel carburetor, and was rated at 310hp.

The 396 was even more impressive when installed in the El Camino. As a car/truck hybrid, the El Camino more closely reflected the sixties muscle car era than any other Chevy truck, and got the big engine before the rest of the pickup line. But even before the 396 option, the El Camino was the top performing truck in the country. As soon as the El Camino was reintroduced for 1964 on a 115in Chevelle wheelbase, it recaptured the high-performance flavor of the earlier, larger El Caminos thanks to the availability of a 230hp 283ci V-8 and a 300hp 327ci V-8. *Car Life* magazine tested both engine combinations and recorded quarter miles times of 16.5 seconds for the 283 and 15.9 seconds for the 327.

Base model, stripped-down trucks had simple block-off plates where the optional radio controls were fitted. An ash tray was located between the radio and ventilation controls.

The 396 pushed the El Camino to even faster acceleration times when it arrived for 1966. The standard SS396 engine developed 325hp, while the optional L34 396 produced a staggering 360hp at 5200rpm—clearly more than was necessary for any freight-hauling duties, but just right for enthusiastic recreational driving. The SS396 package became a staple of the El Camino line, and the optional performance equipment over the years read like a veritable speed catalog. Backing up the big engines were close-ratio or wide-ration four-speed manual transmissions, a Turbo Hydra-Matic automatic, and axle ratios as low as 4.10, 4.56 and 4.88. How fast was an SS396 El Camino? *Car Life* magazine returned to the track in 1968 with a 350hp 396 El Camino and came home with a 14.8 second timeslip.

Large engines and high horsepower ratings were the new developments in the sixties, but most buyers still just needed pickups to be low-cost workers, and the six-cylinder and small V-8 engines remained the most popular. So the challenge for Chevrolet's engineers for the next generation of C-Series trucks, introduced for the 1967 model year, was to keep the design emphasis simple and workmanlike while at the same time trying to satisfy the growing numbers of people who expected more than just steel and vinyl in their pickups.

Most would agree the 1967 models succeeded admirably. The design presented a handsome, squared-off body to the world that looked equally at home at a job site or cruising on Saturday night. Print ads bragged about the styling ("If it looked any better we'd have to stop calling it a truck!"), roomier cab, rust resistant body, and safety features such as a padded dash and sun visor. A new Custom Sport Truck Package helped spruce up the exterior with a chrome bumper and additional bright trim inside and out. Also new that year was an unusual new three-door Suburban. It had one door on the driver's side, and two doors on the passenger's side.

Despite the introduction of the new body style pickups, sales were initially soft and Ford

The 1970 SS396 El Caminos were actually powered by 402ci versions of Chevy's famous big-block engine. The base L34 "396" was rated at 350hp at 5200rpm, the optional L78 rang in at 375hp. With the powerful LS5 454 available (still configured for leaded gas), the 1970 models were the high-water mark for El Camino performance.

A Super Sport package was optional on El Caminos from 1964 until the mid-eighties, making it the longest-lived of all Chevy's various Super Sport models. That may have been a dubious honor though, as in later years the Super Sport option meant little more than tape stripes and spiffier wheels, with no high-performance V-8 to back up the looks.

The SS396 El Camino shared its tough looks with the Chevelle SS series. Prices for the 1970 SS396 El Camino started at $3,305, making it the most expensive light-duty Chevy truck short of 4x4 heavy-duty models.

was able to regain the sales lead over Chevrolet at the end of the decade, although, once again, adding GMC truck totals to Chevrolet totals gave General Motors the lead over Ford Motor Company. (At least until 1970, when a prolonged strike crimped GM production capacity, allowing Ford Motor Co. to overtake total GM truck production for the first time since 1935.)

Another late-sixties development was the introduction of the Chevy Blazer in 1969. The Blazer looked like a shrunken two-door Suburban, but its function in life was to do battle with the smaller Kaiser-Jeep, International Scout and Ford Bronco that were gaining in popularity at the time. The Blazer rode on a 104in wheelbase and was 177.5in long overall,

The Chevy Suburban Carryall was offered in an unusual three-door configuration from 1967 to 1972, with one door on the driver's side, and two on the passenger's side. The 1971 model shown is decked out in DeLuxe trim, which gave the buyer the bright side moldings, full wheel covers, chrome bumpers, and other niceties.

compared to a 90in wheelbase on the Bronco, 101in wheelbase on the Kaiser-Jeep Jeepster Commando, and 100in wheelbase on the Scout. Like the others, the Blazer was available with a removable top, and, initially at least, only in four-wheel drive form. The Blazer, though, benefited from its substantial size advantage, and offered much more powerful, larger engines—

up to the 396ci. Sales were slow initially but grew rapidly, and by the early seventies the Blazer dominated the market segment.

A boost in size was also engineered for the Chevyvan. After years as part of the economical van market in the sixties, Chevy introduced a new full-size van for 1971. The G-Series van went from 90in and 108in wheelbases to a

The Suburban was available with either a traditional tailgate or hinged "ambulance-style" doors. Suburbans were also labeled C-10 or C-20 for one half-and three quarter-ton two-wheel-drive models, or K-10 and K-20 for four-wheel drive. The four-wheel drive option was about $570 on half-ton trucks.

110in wheelbase, and offered a 350ci V-8 option for the first time.

The regular C/K-Series trucks kept their basic shape through 1972, although there were the usual trim changes and upgrades along the way. A 307ci small-block replaced the 283 in 1968, a 350ci V-8 joined the line-up in 1970, and

the 396 was increased to 402ci, although it was labeled a 400. Nineteen-seventy-one was a big year for Chevy trucks, as all pickups were re-engineered to run on unleaded gas, a plain, egg-crate grille replaced the busier designs of earlier years, and front disc brakes brought some much needed stopping ability to the light truck ranks.

The Cheyenne Super option provided higher-level appearance features, such as woodgrain moldings. With black paint, emblems indicating engine displacement, and bucket seats, the Cheyenne Supers foreshadowed the SS454 pickups of the early nineties.

The optional "400" engine in 1972 actually displaced 402ci, and produced 240 net horsepower at 4400rpm. The 402 came standard with a four-barrel carburetor. Compression ratio was a low 8.5:1. More than half of new Chevy buyers were choosing power steering by 1972.

The El Camino continued its association with the Chevelle, following that make's shift to a new body style in 1970. The Chevelle and El Camino both benefited from a brawny, broad-shouldered front end that made the two look more muscular than ever. The wheelbase stayed the same, although overall length increased to 206.8in, within spitting distance of the massive 1959 models. The 250ci six-cylinder was still the standard El Camino engine, with the 307ci V-8, 350ci V-8, 396ci and 454ci big-blocks optional. The engine line-up stayed the same for

1971, although all engines lost power that year as General Motors changed to the lower compression engines compatible with unleaded gas. Power dropped again for 1972, although the 454 was still in the line-up.

As the engine wars subsided in the face of rising insurance costs and increased emission controls (and later the first oil embargo), Chevrolet introduced its first stab at what would quickly travel from a curiosity to an established part of the American truck scene — the compact pickup, in this case the LUV (Light Utility

Checking the Cheyenne Super box brought an upscale interior with woodgrain dash trim, padded headliner, Cheyenne identification on the glovebox, and optional bucket seats with center console. By 1972, around a third of new Chevy trucks were ordered with air conditioning. Only about 7 percent of buyers chose the Cheyenne Super package, according to the *Standard Catalog of American Light Duty Trucks*.

The 1972 C-10 and C-20 continued to be offered in two wheelbases, and two bed lengths.

Vehicle). Manufactured for Chevrolet by Isuzu of Japan, the 1972 LUV relied on a 110ci four-cylinder engine, rated at 75hp. Compact pickups commanded only 5.1 percent of the total U.S. truck market in 1972, but would see a peak of 30.9 percent in 1988 before declining to around 20 percent of the truck market in the nineties.

Ironically, after decades of ever-expanding trucks, with bigger engines and more features, the half-ton LUV rode on a 102in wheelbase and was powered by a four-cylinder engine, just as the first Model 490 half-ton trucks were in 1918. Although few are eager to include the LUV in the pantheon of

LEFT
Hardly standard truck fare in years past, the available tach of the early seventies models shows how far the concept of what a truck should be had traveled. According to the *Standard Catalog of American Light Duty Trucks*, only 2 percent of buyers opted for the tachometer in 1972.

Push button radios had become common by the seventies, although AM/FM was still fairly rare.

great Chevy trucks, it did represent the new industry focus on value and economy, and is a sort of spiritual descendant of the original Model 490, as is the S-10 series introduced in the eighties.

In its own funny way, the LUV did represent the end of one era and the beginning of another. The LUV was at the vanguard of the compact truck explosion in the U.S., joining

Front disc brakes had been made standard equipment on light duty trucks in 1971, and were still a bragging point in 1972. Power brakes were a $50 option.

the Toyota, Datsun, and Ford Courier from Mazda at this new end of the market. The LUV was produced in relatively small numbers, but it pointed the direction for the economical, U.S. built S-10 compact in later years. Although the 1973 full-size pickups would remain large and square, the focus of the following generation would be on aerodynamics and fuel efficiency. The spiraling growth cycle in trucks was no longer a sure thing. Trucks had become a much larger part of everyday life in the United States, and meant a lot of different things to a lot of different people.

Labeled a 400, the 1972 big-block V-8 actually displaced 402ci. With two sixes and four available V-8s, trucks of the early seventies set the tone for the next three decades — buyers expected a choice of engines to meet their various requirements.

4

NEW FRONTIERS

the early 1970s to the early 1990s

The trucks of the 1970s faced more demands than just those imposed by the free market. With a suddenly influential safety lobby, an environmental fever sweeping the nation, and two oil crises brought on by foreign embargoes and foolish domestic regulatory policies, cars and trucks became convenient targets for all manner of legislation designed to clean up the assorted messes.

The basic C/K truck platform introduced in 1973 remained relatively stable through 1987, with one notable facelift in 1981. The best sales year for the series was 1977, when 772,675 full-size Chevys were sold. This series of trucks later caught grief from government officials and activists for "side-saddle" fuel tanks that were mounted outside the frame, although the trucks met existing safety standards and the death rate on the trucks was lower than most competitors'. Shown is a 1986 model. *Chevrolet Division, General Motors Corporation*

Early on, cars took the brunt of the regulatory burdens, with trucks given a bit more breathing room due to the real-life demands placed on working vehicles. The introduction of unleaded gasoline in the early 1970s affected all vehicles, but such requirements as catalytic converters and strict safety standards were not required on all trucks until well after they had been established on cars.

The trends of the decade were guided toward cleaner, safer and more economical transportation, but not much of that was immediately apparent from the introduction of the 1973 full-size Chevy pickups. Larger and heavier than its predecessors, the 1973 C-Series truck also maintained, even amplified, the blocky, square looks of the earlier models. Clearly, aerodynamics and fuel economy were not the overriding design principles of the new truck line. And why should they have been? The government and assorted activists may have wished otherwise, but the public was still

The El Camino soldiered on with the Malibu chassis and drivetrain from 1978-1987, the last of the car/truck hybrids. At the end of the El Camino's run, the only two engine choices were a 4.3 liter V-6 and 5.0 liter V-8. During the last couple years of production, all were assembled in Mexico. Shown is a 1985 model. *Chevrolet Division, General Motors Corporation*

enamored with ever larger, more luxurious, more capable trucks and sport utilities.

The new regular-cab 1973 C- and K-Series trucks rode on 117.5in or 131.5in wheelbases, compared to 115in and 127in the year before. Rear leaf springs replaced coils on 10- and 20-series models. The 454ci V-8, with only 240hp as the result of a low 8.25:1 compression ratio, replaced the 402 as the largest engine in the Chevrolet light truck line. That year also saw the introduction of the one-ton "duallie" with flared rear fenders, and full-time four-wheel drive. One of the first of many safety features to come, an energy-absorbing steering column, was incorporated. The Blazer and Suburban both were switched to the new look at the same time.

The buying public responded enthusiastically in what was an up year for the entire industry. Chevrolet sold 731,176 full-size trucks, a then-record that was eventually surpassed only by 1977 and the industry's all-time record year of 1978 (although additional sales of compact trucks would eventually push total trucks sales well beyond the records set in the 1970s).

The C-Series wasn't the only Chevy truck that received a face lift for 1973. The El Camino also got new sheet metal along with its Chevelle brethren that year. This El Camino was actually slightly smaller overall, but rode on the same 116in wheelbase of the previous year's model. Although physically a bit shorter in length and lower to the ground, there was still no mistaking the El Camino for an economy car. It was 200-300lbs heavier than the 1972s depending on equipment, and maintained its V-8 line-up in 307, 350 and 454ci displacements.

The El Camino's SS option survived through the seventies, although a bit watered down from previous years. Still, with the optional 454 engine an El Camino was an above-average performer. A

1974 El Camino Classic equipped with the 235hp 454 hustled through the quarter mile in 16.5 seconds in a *PV4* magazine road test. The 454 remained an El Camino option through 1975, after which the 400ci small-block survived as the largest available engine. The El Camino offered stacked, dual headlamps on Classic models in 1976, but there were otherwise few changes until the line was redesigned again for 1978.

The big C/K trucks and El Caminos sold well, but the increased demand for economical vehicles had also made room for strong LUV truck sales throughout the 1970s. From 1970 to 1979 compact pickups went from 3.2 percent of the total pickup market to 13.5 percent. The four-cylinder LUV was a big part of that growth. From modest sales of 21,098 in 1972, the LUV achieved sales of 100,192 units in 1979.

The traditional C/K-Series trucks, having proved a success after the 1973 revamping, changed remarkably little over the years. The trucks received a facelift for 1981, but otherwise the basic package stayed unchanged through 1987. Most changes were mechanical upgrades necessary to deal with the evolving fuel economy and emissions regulations, or customary Detroit detail shuffling to differentiate model years. The first catalytic converters on Chevy pickups showed up in 1975, on trucks with a GVW of less than 6,000lbs. GM's electronic HEI (high energy ignition) also joined the line-up for 1975.

Changes for 1977 were mostly visual. Full-size trucks got a cleaner, simpler grille, and a Sport Package option that featured bold (some might say tacky) striping along the truck's sides and hood. White spoke wheels were optional. Detroit's Big Three were closely monitoring the across-the-board rise in truck sales, plus the custom van craze, and all offered loudly-striped sport models in the late-seventies as a way to attract buyers who might

The first-generation S-10 offered everything the bigger trucks did, just on a smaller scale. The S-10 was available with two- or four-wheel drive, regular cab or extended, even as a scaled-down Blazer. All S-10s came with independent front suspension and front disc brakes. *Chevrolet Division, General Motors Corporation*

not have previously considered trucks as sporting transportation. Chevy had the Sport Pickup, Dodge offered a high-performance Little Red Express and a Warlock model, and Ford sold "Free Wheeling" packages with the requisite stripes and custom wheels.

After the first oil embargo washed over the U.S. in 1973, all automakers had scrambled to find ways to improve fuel economy, partly due to market demands and partly due to new CAFE (Corporate Average Fuel Economy) standards from the federal government. One of the first manifestations of GM's attempt to produce economical full-size trucks came in 1978 with the introduction of a 350ci (5.7 liter) V-8 diesel engine option.

Unfortunately, GM's decision to base the new diesel engine off existing gasoline V-8 architecture proved to be a major misstep. The early GM diesels produced much gnashing of teeth and hurling of deleted expletives among the customer base, and many of those early diesels were eventually replaced with gasoline engines. Chevrolet rebounded with a 6.2 liter diesel V-8 in 1982, an engine of sturdier design that earned back many of the diesel customers lost by the earlier effort. The 6.2 produced 130hp at 3600rpm and 240lb-ft of torque at 2000rpm, compared to the 125hp/225 lb-ft of the 5.7 diesel.

Chevy's other stab at a more economical truck in 1978 came with the introduction of a new, downsized El Camino. This new El Camino was nearly a foot shorter and 600lbs lighter than the 1973-77 models, and offered a 200ci V-6 as the standard engine. Optional engines included a second V-6, at 231ci displacement, a 305ci V-8 and a 350ci V-8. In a further attempt to find that elusive compromise between performance and economy, a 267ci version of Chevy's durable small-block was introduced in the El Camino in 1979. Both underpowered and somewhat less than truly economi-

cal, the engine was not the magic compromise some at Chevrolet might have hoped.

The next exterior freshening of full-size trucks came in 1981. The '81 models were given a more flush, aerodynamic nose, with quad headlamps and the parking lamps integrated into the front bumper. Along with the new aerodynamic face, Chevy engineers carved some weight out of the big trucks, leading to some slight improvements in fuel economy.

Although worthy improvements, the second oil "crisis" of 1979 and a rapidly worsening recession choked off full-size trucks sales in the early eighties. Chevy sold fewer than 400,000 C/K-Series trucks in 1982, the worst showing since the early 1960s. Chevrolet's response to the shifts in the market arrived just in time for 1982, however, in the form of the compact S-10 pickups.

The Chevy S-10 and its twin GMC S-15 were GM's domestic answers to the wave of imported compact trucks that had made such quick gains in the U.S. market. Based on either a 108.3in or 118in wheelbase, the S-10 weighed in at less than 3,000lbs and was powered by a miserly 1.9 liter four-cylinder engine. Unlike the Japanese competition, though, Chevrolet offered a V-6 engine option. The 2.8-liter (173ci) six produced 110hp and 148lb-ft of torque, good for that class of truck.

The S-10 also differed from its import competition in the looks department. The S-Series styling was clearly influenced by the larger C/K-Series trucks, rather than Japanese compact trucks of similar mission. The look was square and clean, and obviously American in origin. GM may have wanted to play in the same pool as the imports, but they also wanted to transfer the goodwill earned from generations of well-received bigger trucks onto the diminutive new S-Series. The effort paid off, as Chevy sold 177,758 S-10s that first year.

93

The 454SS Chevy truck was produced from 1990 to 93. Its best sales year was 1990, when 13,748 were sold. The SS had reduced payload capacity, a high price tag and only got 10-12mpg, but most buyers forgot all that once they got behind the wheel. The 454SS was a pure thrill machine, good for quarter mile times in the mid- to high-15 second range. Its mid-range punch was even better. *Chevrolet Division, General Motors Corporation*

The success of the S-10 made the LUV superfluous, and it was dropped from the Chevrolet line-up after 1982.

Compact trucks were where the action was in the early eighties, and Chevrolet wasted little time upgrading the S-10 and expanding the choice of body styles to take advantage of that trend. Chevy introduced both extended cab and Blazer versions

of the S-10 for 1983. The S-10 Blazer was a good complement to the full-size Blazer, offering much of the image without so much of the bulk. Sales were even better in 1983, with 198,222 S-10 trucks sold, plus 106,214 S-10 Blazers. A 2.0 liter four cylinder joined the line-up that year.

The S-10 continued to evolve throughout the 1980s. A hydraulic clutch replaced the cable type clutch for 1984, and a Sport suspension was added that same year. Gas shocks replaced hydraulic units on some models. A larger, more powerful 2.5 liter fuel-injected four-cylinder engine was inserted into the line-up in 1985, and the 2.8 V-6 was fuel injected the year after that. In 1988, Chevrolet created a 4.3 liter V-6 by cutting off two cylinders from the venerable 350ci V-8, giving the S-10 and Blazer 160 horses to play with.

While an important part of Chevrolet's truck arsenal, the S-10 was still secondary in sales and image to the full-size trucks, and the corporation wasn't about to let the big rigs languish. With their 1988 re-do, the C/K-Series trucks were the first full-size American trucks to get a fully modern aero treatment. GM clearly got the drop on Ford and Dodge with the new trucks, which featured not only aerodynamic styling but class-leading ride and handling. The new trucks utilized flush glass, a sloping hood and rounded front end, and a narrower body to cut a cleaner path through the wind. Body options included a regular cab or extended cab, 6.5ft or 8ft bed, in Fleetside or Sportside configurations. The improved ride was thanks to a new chassis and independent, double A-arm front suspension. The powertrain roll call included a base 4.3 liter V-6, 5.0 liter V-8, 5.7 liter V-8, 7.4 liter V-8 and 6.2 liter V-8 diesel. The interior was also all-new, with gauges that reminded one of digital readouts—perhaps the least successfully executed area of the trucks, but at least distinctive.

Given the ferocious nature of the nineties' truck market, Chevrolet has had little room to sit on its laurels. Fortunately, the C/K-series trucks have continued to evolve. A true high-performance 454SS model was added in 1990. A crew cab was mated to the new style in 1992, along with a Sportside Box

CPC MARK V
7.4L – V8 FUEL INJECTED

The 454SS engine produced 230 hp and 385 lb-ft of torque when introduced in 1990. The engine was reworked in 1992, and tuned to 255hp and 405lb-ft of torque. *Chevrolet Division, General Motors Corporation*

for extended cab models. A powerful and smooth 6.5 liter turbo diesel V-8 also came on line in 1992. After a few years delay, the Blazer and Suburban were switched over to the new style in 1992 as well.

Remarkably, despite added competition, the American truck market continues to expand and GM trucks sales are flourishing at all-time highs. Trucks are integrated into American's lifestyles more than ever. Sport Utilities have replaced station wagons, and pickups have established themselves as ideal daily transportation for millions. NASCAR has even sanctioned a SuperTruck racing series so Chevys, Fords and Dodges can bang fenders at tracks across the country — and has met with immediate success. As this is written, trucks hold 42.6 percent of the new vehicle market, with no signs of let-up in sight. It just may come to pass that trucks are the majority vehicles in this country, and Chevrolet may very well rule that roost.

INDEX